## Educators Love STEP-UP Books.
## So Do Children.*

**In this exciting series:**

- THE WORDS ARE HARDER (but not too hard)
- THERE'S A LOT MORE TEXT (but it's in bigger print)
- THERE ARE PLENTY OF ILLUSTRATIONS (but they are not just picture books)
- And the subject matter has been carefully chosen to appeal to young readers who want to find out about the world for themselves. These informative and lively books are just the answer.

### *"STEP-UP BOOKS

. . . fill a need for precise informational material written in a simple readable form which children can and will enjoy. More please!"—EVELYN L. HEADLEY, *Director of Elementary Education, Edison, New Jersey.*
"I love them."—STEVE MEYER, *second grade pupil, Chicago, Illinois.*

**REPTILES DO THE STRANGEST THINGS.** The hog-nose snake rolls over and plays dead. The draco lizard flies from tree to tree. And a big underwater turtle uses his tongue as a bait to catch fish. All these and many other strange reptile antics are here, in this latest book in the Step-Up nature series. The illustrations are as accurate as they are entertaining, and all the facts are true.

# REPTILES
## do the
# STRANGEST
# THINGS

by
Leonora and Arthur Hornblow

Illustrations by Michael K. Frith

Step-Up Books ⌐_⌐ Random House
New York

# For Scott and Tony Shepherd

LEONORA & ARTHUR HORNBLOW are the co-authors of five books in the unique Step-Up nature series: *Animals Do the Strangest Things, Birds Do the Strangest Things, Fish Do the Strangest Things, Insects Do the Strangest Things* and *Reptiles Do the Strangest Things*.

Arthur Hornblow, Jr. is best known as the movie producer who made such famous films as *Oklahoma, Weekend at the Waldorf, Gaslight* and *Witness for the Prosecution*.

Leonora Hornblow is a columnist, novelist, and author of historical books for children.

The Hornblows live in New York City where they are Associate Members of the American Museum of Natural History and the New York Zoological Society.

MICHAEL K. FRITH is from Bermuda and is a Harvard graduate. At Harvard he majored in Fine Arts, and was president of the *Harvard Lampoon*. He has since illustrated all of the Hornblows' nature books and several books for adults.

Mr. Frith, his wife and children live in New York, where he works as an illustrator, designer and editor of children's books.

This title was originally catalogued by the Library of Congress as follows: Hornblow, Leonora. Reptiles do the strangest things, by Leonora and Arthur Hornblow. Illus. by Michael K. Frith. Random House [c1970] 60 p. illus. (Step-up books) A brief look at the habits, characteristics, physical appearance, behavioral patterns and environments of different types of reptiles around the world. 1. Reptiles—Habits and behavior. I. Title. B 36-814   598.1   ISBN 0-394-80074-5   ISBN 0-394-90074-X  (lib. bdg.)

# Contents

# REPTILES DO THE STRANGEST THINGS

The Time

# of the Monsters

Millions and millions of years ago
there lived a huge animal called a
Brontosaurus. He was as long as a
line of ten elephants and weighed
over 75,000 pounds. He was so big
he could hardly move around on land.
He spent his days wading in the
water, eating green plants.

The Brontosaurus was a dinosaur.
Dinosaurs were reptiles. They ruled
the earth for millions of years.

There were dinosaurs as small as rabbits. There were dinosaurs as tall as a four-story building. A terrible kind of dinosaur called the Tyrannosaurus Rex had a huge head and a thousand teeth. He could kill and eat a Brontosaurus.

Tyrannosaurus Rex means "king of the lizard tyrants." Brontosaurus means "thunder lizard." Dinosaur means "terrible lizard."

These fantastic reptiles all died long before there were any people on earth. So no one ever saw a dinosaur. But today we know about them from their bones.

Dinosaur bones have been found buried in rocks in many parts of the world. You can see these bones in museums. In one, there is a giant skeleton of a Tyrannosaurus Rex. Even without his skin he is scary.

Today there are only five kinds of reptiles. They are the Lizards, the Turtles, the Snakes, the Crocodilians, and an odd animal called the Tuatara.

# I'm Left Over

There are many kinds of snakes and turtles. There are many kinds of crocodilians and lizards. But there is only one kind of tuatara.

Over the millions of years, all the other reptiles of his kind died away. The small tuatara is a leftover from the days of the dinosaurs.

This strange little leftover breathes very slowly. Sometimes a tuatara may not take a breath for an hour!

And the eggs of the female tuatara hatch very slowly, too. The babies don't come out for at least a year.

Tuataras are found in only one part of the world. They live in small islands off New Zealand. On these islands live many sea birds called petrels. The petrels dig burrows in the sandy earth. Then a strange thing happens. The tuataras move right in with the petrels.

A tuatara can dig his own burrow. Why does he move in with the petrels? Maybe even a leftover likes company.

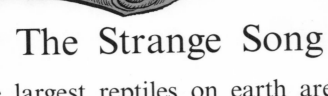

# The Strange Song

The largest reptiles on earth are the crocodilians. These are crocodiles, alligators and their cousins.

Large or small, most reptiles are strangely silent. Some have no voices at all. But the "song of the crocodilian" is one of the loudest sounds in the animal world. The mighty roar of a big crocodile rolls like thunder through the swamp.

Crocodilians live in swamps near rivers and oceans. They love water.

All of them are strong swimmers.
They catch and eat most of their
food right in the water.

A crocodile drifts slowly down the
river. He hardly makes a ripple.
Only his eyes and the tip of his nose
are above the water. He can breathe
and see without being seen. He is
watching and waiting for his prey.
It might be a bug. It might be a fish.
Or it might be a big animal.

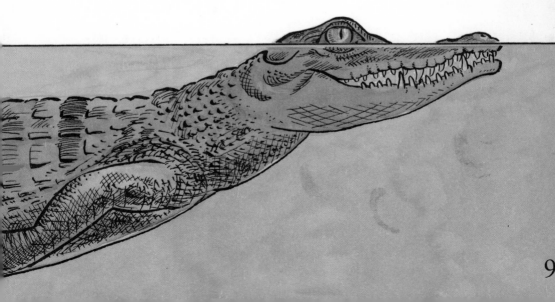

Often the big crocodiles wait for
animals to come to the water to drink.
Then the crocs may swing their tails
and knock their prey into the water.
Or they may grab an animal by the
nose with their jaws and pull it in.
This is how African crocodiles catch
deer, pigs and sometimes even cows.

The jaws of big crocodilians are
so strong they can crush a man.
But some men wrestle with alligators!
At "animal farms" in Florida you can
see these strange wrestling matches.
The terrible teeth of the reptiles look
very frightening. But an alligator
cannot bite if his mouth is held shut.

So the men just hold the toothy jaws closed and pretend to wrestle. They may even have to shake the alligators' heads to make the fight look dangerous. The poor 'gators probably just want to get away.

Alligators build wonderful nests for their eggs. First the mother bites wet leaves and branches from nearby bushes. Then she pushes them into a big pile. With her back feet she digs a hollow in the pile. There she lays her eggs. Now she covers the pile with mud and damp plants.

With her belly she smooths the top and closes the nest. The mother may have to work for three days and nights to build this nest. But her eggs will be safe and warm.

The mother alligator doesn't forget her eggs. She comes back often to fix the nest. In about nine weeks she hears little peeping noises. This means the eggs inside are ready to hatch. She tears open the nest and helps her babies to come out.

Baby alligators are sometimes sold as pets. This is very cruel. Most of them soon die. People kill the big crocodilians and sell their skins. Now very few of them are left in the swamps. It is sad to think that the thundering "song of the croc" may someday be heard only at the zoo.

# The Wonderful Serpents

In old stories and legends you may read about serpents. That is just another name for snakes. There are short snakes and long snakes. There are thin snakes and fat snakes. There are snakes that can swim a thousand miles out to sea.

There are snakes that fly from tree to tree.

Some snakes curl themselves up into a ball.

One kind of snake can spit poison right in people's eyes.

Another kind can catch a bat flying through the air.

Many people don't know that snakes can do such wonderful things. Some think that all snakes are dangerous and slimy. But very few snakes hurt men. And no snake is slimy. The skin of a snake is clean and soft.

Babies like to play with snakes and pat their shiny skins. Some snakes make nice pets. But look out! Some of the wonderful serpents can be dangerous.

# The Dangerous Rattle

Dogs bark. Birds sing. Pigs grunt. But only one creature on earth can rattle its tail. This is the famous rattlesnake. On his tail he has a built-in rattle. When he is angry or frightened he rattles it.

A baby rattler has no rattle. He has only a tiny button on his tail. But in every other way he is like a grown-up rattlesnake. Baby rattlers can take care of themselves as soon as they are born. Their mother does nothing to help them. Each baby must hunt for his own food.

Rattlers are born with special teeth called fangs. When they bite, poison comes through these fangs. The poison is called venom. A young rattler has very little venom. His bite cannot kill a man. But it can kill a mouse.

A week or two after he is born, the rattler does a strange thing. He rubs his nose and mouth against a stone. He rubs until he makes a little hole in his skin. Slowly he pushes himself through the hole. He wriggles right out of his own skin! Under the old skin is a nice new one.

17

He moves away and leaves the old skin on the ground. This is something he will do about three times a year for the rest of his life.

All snakes shed their skin in this way. Even the clear covering over their eyes come off. In the old skin this covering looks just like a pair of eyeglasses.

Every time the rattler sheds, a ring of dry skin stays around the button on his tail. As the snake grows, the rattle grows, too. The larger the snake the larger the rattle.

Someday you may hear that rattle.
If you do, get away fast! It means
a rattlesnake is curled up near
by. He is lashing
his tail, ready to
strike. But he will
not strike unless
you come too close
and frighten him.

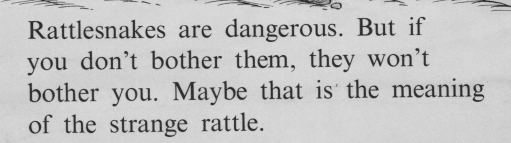

Rattlesnakes are dangerous. But if
you don't bother them, they won't
bother you. Maybe that is the meaning
of the strange rattle.

# The Game of Death

The hog-nose is a gentle snake. He has no rattle. He has no venom. He never bites. When an enemy is near he does a funny thing. He puffs up his body, lashes his tail and hisses. If the enemy won't go away, the hog-nose tries a new trick. He rolls over and plays dead. Then he peeks to see if it is safe to move. If someone flips him over, he flips right back. He probably thinks he looks more dead upside down.

# The Great Swallow

Almost everybody likes to eat eggs.
In Africa there is a snake that eats
nothing else. It isn't easy. Often
the eggs are twice as wide as he is.

The egg-eater opens his mouth very
wide. He stretches it over an egg.
Slowly the egg slides in. He closes
his mouth. For a moment he looks
like a little watermelon. Then the
egg reaches sharp bones in his
throat. These bones cut the shell.
The egg slides down. The snake spits
out the shell. Nobody, not even an
egg-eater, likes to eat eggshells.

# The Dancer in a Basket

In India men called snake-charmers make snakes dance. Their favorite dancing snake is the king cobra.

A snake-charmer puts a basket down on the street. He sits by it and plays a flute. Suddenly a cobra's head comes up. The big serpent hisses. He leans towards the man. But the wise charmer moves away. He knows that the venom in a cobra's bite could kill him.

The cobra watches as the charmer
plays the flute. Soon the skin below
the snake's head begins to flatten
and spread. This odd swelling is
called the hood of the cobra. It is
a sign that the cobra is angry. Now
the hooded snake sways back and
forth. He seems to be dancing to the
music. But he is only following the
moving flute. Like all snakes, the
cobra is deaf. The beautiful dancer
can't even hear the music.

# The Big Squeeze

The giants of the snake world are the python and the anaconda. Both can grow to be over 30 feet long. Some are as big around as a telephone pole.

In the jungles of Burma big pythons live among the trees. They wind their heavy bodies around the branches. They crawl along the jungle trails. Sometimes they crawl into a village and terrify the natives. But they rarely eat people. They eat birds and small animals. The biggest pythons often eat deer and wild pigs.

Pythons and anacondas have no venom. They have another way of killing. They twist their bodies around their prey. They squeeze and squeeze. Soon the victim stops breathing. Then they eat him.

A python kills a wild pig. Then he grabs its head with his many teeth. Slowly he pulls himself over his prey. Little by little the pig goes in. And soon the python has an enormous middle. After such a big meal he may not eat again for a year.

Pythons and anacondas cannot tear their victims apart. So they must swallow them whole. This may seem hard. But all snakes have jaws that open very wide. A giant anaconda can swallow a six-foot crocodilian.

On the banks of the Amazon River an anaconda wraps himself around a crocodilian. He pins the croc against a tree. Then he squeezes him to death.

Anacondas are great swimmers. They live in rivers. They even give birth to living babies right in the water. The babies are over three feet long. And they can already swim.

Baby pythons come out of eggs. The mother python does something no other snake does. She coils herself around the eggs until they hatch. But when the babies hatch she won't take care of them. They must take care of themselves. They already know how to hunt. And no one has to teach a python how to use the "big squeeze."

# A House on his Back

Only one kind of reptile carries his house on his back. That is the wonderful turtle. He is born with a soft covering of shell and bone. As he grows it hardens and grows, too. He will wear the shell all his life. It will keep him safe from enemies.

If an enemy comes near, the turtle acts fast. He pulls in his head. He pulls in his tail. He pulls up his legs. And he won't come out until he wants to. No one can make him.

There are turtles that live in the
water and turtles that live on land.
Water turtles don't always stay in
the water. Often many of them climb
up on rocks or logs to sit in the sun.

Some people have turtles for pets.
The box turtle makes a good pet. He
is very well named. His top shell and
bottom shell fit tightly together. And
when he pulls his legs in, flaps
close up each side. But if he eats
too much, he gets too big for his box.
Then his fat legs keep popping out.

# The Big Snap

Turtles have no teeth. They have beaks. They use them to catch their food and tear it apart.

One kind of turtle has a very sharp beak. And his strong jaws snap. He is the mean snapping turtle. Most turtles are gentle. If an enemy is near they hide in their shells. Not the snapper. He snaps and bites.

If you meet a snapper, don't pick him up. He might think you're an enemy and snap at you.

The biggest and ugliest snappers are the alligator snapping turtles. They can grow to be over 200 pounds. They live on muddy river bottoms.

An alligator snapper has a strange way of catching fish. He lies on the river bed with his mouth wide open. He looks like a lump of mud. Fish may not see him. But they see his tongue. It looks like a tiny pink worm. He wiggles his tongue. A fish swims in to get the bait. The snapper snaps. What a lazy way to get dinner!

# The Soft One

In America, turtles that live on land are called tortoises. Tortoises have rounder, higher shells than water turtles. They like to eat plants. They go to water only to drink or bathe.

In Africa there is an odd reptile called Tornier's tortoise. He can do something few other turtles can do. If he falls on his back he can flip himself over. But his shell is too soft to keep him safe from enemies. When he is afraid he crawls into a crack between rocks. He puffs himself up. Now no enemy can get him.

# The Land Giants

On faraway islands in the Pacific Ocean live the biggest of all the tortoises. These are the Galapagos tortoises. Their thick legs look almost like the legs of elephants. These huge reptiles live to a very old age. One is known to have lived for more than 152 years.

Some Galapagos tortoises may weigh over 500 pounds. If you see a big one at the zoo, you may have a chance to ride on him.

# The Sea Giants

Some of the turtles that live in the sea are giants, too. They are the green turtles. They can be as long as a man and five times as heavy.

Sea turtles are fine swimmers. They do not have legs like land turtles. They have flippers. These help them to move through the water. Of all the turtles, the best swimmers are the green giants of the sea.

Sea turtles spend all their lives
in the water. They eat and sleep in
the water. But there is one thing
they have to do on land. The turtles
of the sea must come up on beaches
to lay their eggs.

On a moonlit night a mother turtle
crawls slowly up the sand. It is
hard for her to walk on her flippers.
She does something very strange.
She pushes her flippers through
the sand as if she were swimming.
It takes her a long time to drag her
heavy body up the beach. Sometimes
she stops and lets out a huge sigh.

The green turtle waddles along the beach looking for a spot she likes. At last she finds a dry place high above the water. With her front flippers she scoops out a bed for herself. Behind the bed she digs a hole. Now she begins to lay her eggs. Soon there may be as many as 100 eggs in the hole. They look like a pile of ping-pong balls. Then the big turtle covers the eggs with sand. Slowly she waddles back to the sea. She will never see her eggs again.

In two or three months the baby
turtles come out of their shells.
Now they must get to the sea. No
one is there to show them where to
go. Somehow they just know. They
run right for the water. But many
of these little turtlets will never
reach the sea. Their shells are not
yet hard enough to protect them.
Birds wait overhead to swoop down
and eat them. Animals on the beach
run after them. And even if they
get to the sea they may not be safe.
Big fish may eat them. It's lucky
for green turtles that the mother
turtle lays so many eggs.

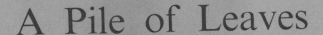

# A Pile of Leaves

Some people think a matamata is the oddest looking creature in the world. He surely is the oddest looking turtle. His shell is covered with bumps. Sticking to the bumps are many tiny green plants. The matamata looks like a pile of rubbish and leaves.

On a shallow river bottom in South America, a matamata sits waiting. He stretches his long neck up out of the water. He takes a breath through his strange snorkel nose.

Then he pulls his head back under the water. He is hungry. His tiny eyes watch for fish. Suddenly a group of fish swim over. They try to eat some bits from the rubbish pile. But they don't eat. They get eaten. The matamata just opens his enormous mouth. Swoosh! A great load of water rushes in. A fish gets swept in, too. Then the matamata spits out the water. But he doesn't spit out the fish!

# Little Clown

There are almost 3,000 kinds of
lizards. They come in many colors
and sizes. They do many odd things.

Most lizards have no voices at all.
But the merry little gecko squeaks
and squeals. And he says "Gecko-
gecko." That is how he got his name.

Geckos are found in warm countries.
Some kinds like to live in people's
houses. The people who have geckos
are lucky. Their little lizards will
run around eating up roaches,
mosquitoes and many other pests.

It is fun to see geckos running around the house. They are pretty. Their eyes are big and bright. If you talk to them, they seem to listen. But watch out! If you pick up a gecko, you may get a surprise. He might run away—and leave you holding his tail. Geckos can drop off their tails whenever they want to. It doesn't matter. They can grow new ones. Sometimes a tail breaks but doesn't fall off. Then the old tail grows back on again and a new tail grows beside it. Some geckos even have three tails.

Geckos are great climbers. They can run up and down walls. Some kinds can even run across a ceiling. These geckos have special pads on their feet. On the bottom of each pad are many tiny, tiny hooks. The strange pads are not sticky. But they can cling to almost anything. A gecko with these pads on his feet can walk right up a glass window.

In Malaysia some boys use the gecko's remarkable feet to play tricks. They tie a string around a big gecko's neck. They carry him up to the roof of a low building.

There they wait until a man comes down the street. Then they lean over and dangle the gecko above his head. The gecko's feet grab onto the man's hat. The boys quickly pull the string. Up comes the gecko. Off comes the hat.

# The Great Escapers

Like geckos, skinks can drop off
their tails. Some of these lizards
have tiny legs. Some have no legs
at all. They don't run when they are
frightened. They slide away like
snakes. In fact, people may think
they are snakes. But skinks have
ears and eyelids. Snakes have not.

Skinks live in many places. Often
they are brightly colored. But they
are seldom seen. These shy lizards
hide under stones and leaves. If you
come near, they quickly wiggle away.

# The Magic Tail

Of all the lizards only two kinds have venom. These dangerous reptiles are the Mexican beaded lizard and his cousin, the Gila monster.

The Gila monster doesn't like the heat. He sleeps in the day. When the sun goes down he goes out to hunt for eggs and helpless baby animals.

The Gila has an odd way of storing food. When he eats a lot his tail gets fat. Then he can stop eating. His body slowly uses up the fat. After several months the Gila may not be hungry. But he has a very thin tail.

# The Blood-Squirter

The horned toad looks like a toad.
He often acts like a toad. He is
called a toad. But he is not a toad.
He is a member of the lizard family.

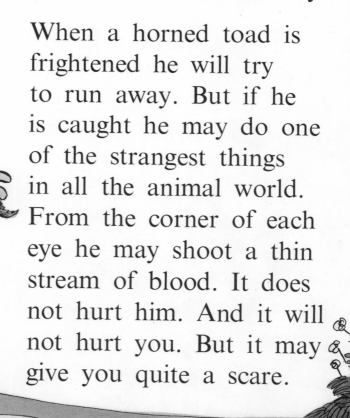

When a horned toad is
frightened he will try
to run away. But if he
is caught he may do one
of the strangest things
in all the animal world.
From the corner of each
eye he may shoot a thin
stream of blood. It does
not hurt him. And it will
not hurt you. But it may
give you quite a scare.

Horned toads live in desert country. Most desert animals hide from the sun. Not the horned toads. They stay out in the blazing sun chasing insects. When the sun goes down, the desert gets cool. To keep warm, the horned toads do another strange thing. They stick their heads in the sand. Then they flip sand over their bodies. Soon they are wrapped in little overcoats of sand. When the big animals come out to hunt in the dark, they won't find any horned toads. The little lizards will be safe in their sandy beds.

# The Smoke-Puffer

The big marine iguanas are the best swimmers of all the lizards. They spend all their time by the sea.

They live on the beaches and rocks of the Galapagos Islands. There they may lie in the sun for hours. They wait for the water to go down as the tide goes out. Then they crawl slowly down to the water to look for their favorite food—seaweed.

Marine iguanas are angry-looking
reptiles. They have tough, flat faces.
Along their backs are strange, sharp
spines. And when people come near
them, they do an amazing thing.
They puff a kind of steam through
their noses. This may look scary.
But the marine iguanas are really
very shy. They just like to sit
together on their rocks by the sea.

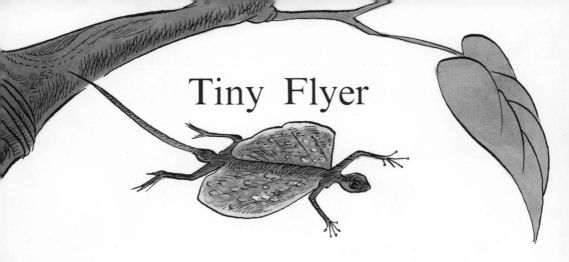

# Tiny Flyer

The draco is a tiny lizard. But he
can do something no big lizard can
do. At each side of his thin little
body are flaps of folded skin. These
flaps lie flat when the draco runs
along the ground or climbs a tree.
Then he looks like a small green
twig. But if he jumps off a branch,
the brightly colored flaps open out.
They look like beautiful wings. And
the little draco glides like a bird
from tree to tree.

# The Beautiful Frill

In Australia there is a wonderful reptile called the frilled lizard. Around his neck is a fold of loose skin. It lies flat when he isn't using it. But if he sees an enemy he spreads out the fold. A great frill opens behind his head like a big umbrella. The frilled lizard stands up on his back legs and shows his teeth. Suddenly he looks big and mean. If he's lucky his act will frighten his enemy away. What a strange way to use a pretty frill!

# The Water-Walker

The basilisk has no frill. But he has a crest along his back and tail. His tail is long and thin and very strong. And sometimes he uses it to help him run. He can run fast. He can climb trees. Strangest of all, this funny lizard can walk on water. When the basilisk is frightened, he gets up on his back legs and runs.

He swings from side to side. His long tail helps to keep his balance. If he comes to a stream he runs right over it. He may get tired and sink into the water. But that's all right. The basilisk can swim, too.

# The Color-Changers

A little lizard called the "American chameleon" is really a Carolina anole. He does a wonderful thing. He changes color! When he is angry or afraid, he changes. If the air gets colder or warmer, he changes. If the light grows brighter or darker, he changes again. The anole also has a special pouch of skin on his throat. When he spreads it open it looks like a bright pink fan. Sometimes he uses this fan to show off to a lady anole. More often he uses it to scare away other males.

Wild anoles live in trees. There they eat insects and sleep on twigs among the leaves. But people sometimes catch anoles. They sell them at pet shops and fairs. If you ever buy an anole, remember that he is used to living in a tree. He may not know how to drink from a dish. Just sprinkle a few drops of·water on a leaf. Then he may feel more at home. And you can watch the nice little color-changer changing color.

Another color-changer is the true chameleon. He is one of the oddest of all the reptiles. He can change from brown to green and back to brown again. Sometimes part of him is in the sun and part in the shade. Then he's two colors at once! This queer lizard has bumpy skin, pop eyes and a tail that rolls up in a curl. He may have a horn on his head. He might even have three. And his tongue can be longer than his whole body.

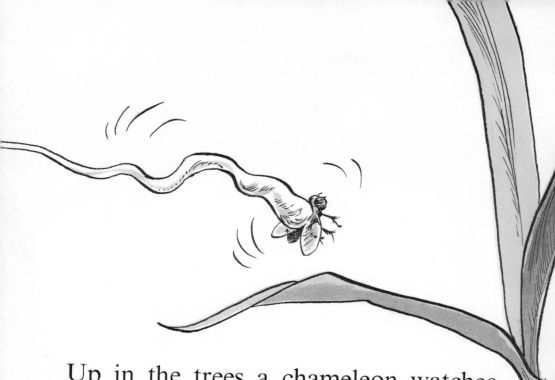

Up in the trees a chameleon watches
for insects. He rolls one eye forward
and one back. He can see ahead or
behind at the same time. Along comes
a bug. The chameleon shoots out his
fantastic tongue. On its tip is some
sticky stuff. The tongue hits the
bug. The bug sticks. The chameleon
pulls in his tongue. Zip! No bug.

# A Monster of Today

Far away in the warm Indian Ocean is the island of Komodo. There live the largest lizards on earth. They are the Komodo Dragons. These giant lizards can be ten feet long. The biggest ones weigh over 300 pounds.

Komodo Dragons can climb trees. It is strange to see a five-foot Dragon sitting up among the branches. But the Dragons spend most of their time on the ground.

A Komodo Dragon moves slowly
through the high grass. His heavy body
moves from side to side. His long
yellow tongue flicks in and out. He
is hunting for food. Like snakes,
the Dragon picks up smells in the
air with his tongue. He looks for
a dead animal. If he doesn't find
one, he kills a wild pig, a deer or
a goat. Then he has a messy feast.
He bites off big chunks of meat and
swallows them whole.

The Komodo Dragon is a strange beast indeed. As he flicks his yellow tongue, he looks like the dragon of fairy tales and legends.

We know there are no real dragons.

And no one ever saw a live dinosaur.

But there are many creatures that are almost as strange. And among the strangest are the remarkable reptiles that still share our earth.

# The
# STEP-UP Books

## NATURE LIBRARY

**ANIMALS DO THE STRANGEST THINGS**
**BIRDS DO THE STRANGEST THINGS**
**FISH DO THE STRANGEST THINGS**
**INSECTS DO THE STRANGEST THINGS**
**REPTILES DO THE STRANGEST THINGS**

## Story of AMERICA

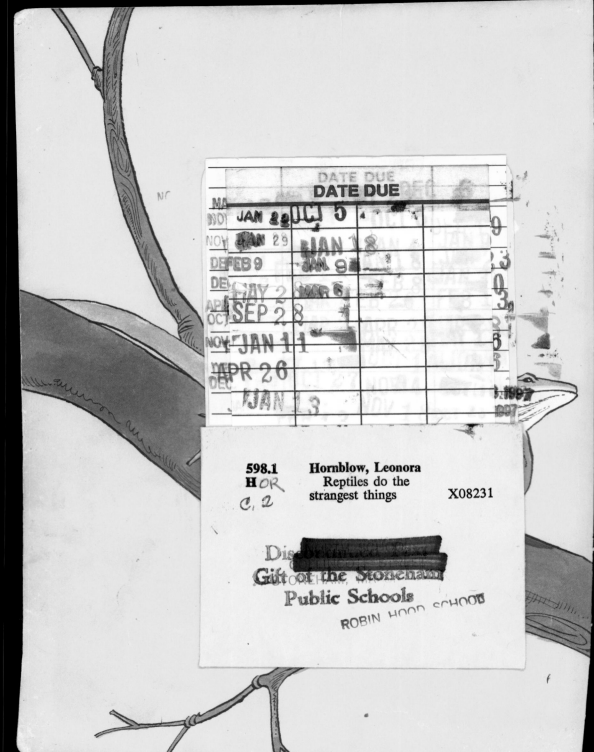